Eulogies

For Those We Lost To

Sudden Illness:

Writing Guidelines, Examples, And

Templates

With Tips For Grieving, Healing And
Moving On

J Jordan

Notable+

Copyright & Disclaimer

EULOGIES FOR THOSE WE LOST TO SUDDEN ILLNESS: WRITING GUIDELINES, EXAMPLES, AND TEMPLATES

Eulogies For Those We Lost To Sudden Illness: Writing Guidelines, Examples, and Templates
Paperback: 103 Pages
Print Quality: Black ink and 55# (90 GSM) cream paper
ISBN-10: 1-960176-14-5
ISBN-13: 978-1-960176-14-1

Contents

Preface

Firstly, please accept my deepest condolences. Losing a loved one is an incredibly challenging experience, and I sincerely pray that you find the strength to endure during this time of immense pain and loss.

Honoring The Memory Of Loved Ones Lost To Sudden Illness

The sudden loss of a loved one due to illness can leave us grappling with a profound mix of emotions. In the midst of sorrow, it becomes crucial to remember the joy and celebrate the life they lived. This book aims to provide guidance and solace for those navigating the complexities of mourning an individual who passed away unexpectedly due to illness. By exploring ways to capture their essence, honor their legacy, and embrace joyful remembrance, we can find healing amidst grief and craft a heartfelt eulogy. Additionally, we will delve into the significance of community support, meaningful rituals of remembrance, celebration of life, and ultimately finding hope as we move forward. Although the pain may seem overwhelming, it is indeed possible to remember the joy amidst sorrow, keeping the spirit of our loved ones alive in our hearts.

Finding Strength Amidst Sudden Loss

When news of the passing of a loved one arrives, and you find yourself overwhelmed with emotions while simultaneously planning the funeral and holding the rest of the family together, writing a eulogy becomes an arduous task. The raw and gut-wrenching thoughts of your loved one being gone make it challenging to create a eulogy that truly honors their memory. Moreover, amidst all the chaos, you must gather the courage to stand before an audience of grieving individuals, paying tribute to the deceased and offering words of encouragement to those in mourning. The weight of this responsibility can feel like an additional burden atop the mountain of challenges you already face.

However, it is a task that must be undertaken, and if you are reading this, it means that this great responsibility has been entrusted to you. I have personally experienced the position you find yourself in right now, and I wholeheartedly empathize with your situation. Despite the overwhelming emotions you may be experiencing, I firmly believe that you possess bravery and courage, even if you may not feel it at this moment. And you will accomplish this task of honoring your dearly departed.

About Eulogies

The eulogy is a distinct type of speech due to many factors; mainly the purpose, the occasion and the mental and emotional state of the audience. It requires a different approach and this book is specifically designed to assist you in this particular task. It is not a generic speech writing guide, as that is not what you need at this moment. The intention is not to delve deep into the mechanics of speech writing, but rather to help you structure your eulogy with all the requisite parts in a clear introduction, body and conclusion.

Furthermore, the body of the eulogy contains crucial sections. These sections are included and can be customized to suit your specific requirements. Within the eulogies presented in this book, you will find introductions, conclusions, and segments dedicated to sharing cherished memories, highlighting the deceased's passions, discussing their influence, and offering words of comfort to those attending the funeral.

Eulogies employ specific language and sections that enable us to convey the sentiments we wish to express. During grief, it can be difficult to find the right words and structure that communicate our emotions while paying tribute to someone who held great significance in our lives. Fortunately, this book provides the words and structure for you.

The Purpose Of This Book

This book offers practical examples and templates to aid your eulogy writing and serves as a guide to help you navigate the grieving process. You can largely copy, modify, and adapt these resources to suit the eulogy you are preparing. Its purpose is to alleviate some of the difficulties associated with this task during such a challenging time.

While these eulogies can serve as sources of inspiration, it is important to personalize your tribute to reflect the unique life and relationship you shared with your loved one. Use the structure and themes highlighted here as guides, but make sure to incorporate your own memories, anecdotes, and emotions to create a heartfelt eulogy that truly honors your loved one.

Sections, Fields And FAQ

Sections
This book offers a variety of eulogy sections that you can customize and incorporate into your eulogy. The language used in these sections is in line with the common expressions found in eulogies. By eliminating the need to fret over the wording or search for the perfect phrases to express your emotions, writing eulogies becomes a less daunting task.

Fields

Specific fields, such as [Name], are used to conveniently accommodate the inclusion of relevant information about the deceased. These fields assist in personalizing and the eulogies to honor your loved one.

Tips

Italicized tips are a valuable component designed to ignite creativity and motivation within your writing endeavors. These carefully curated suggestions serve as a catalyst for inspiration and the exploration of new ideas.

Prompts

These words serve as a compass for your writing endeavors urging you to include captivating stories, cherished memories, and entertaining anecdotes.

FAQ

The Frequently Asked Questions (FAQ) section provides comprehensive answers to common inquiries regarding writing eulogies, as well as coping with loss, healing, and moving forward.

Once again, I extend my deepest condolences to you and your loved ones during this time of need. I sincerely pray that you find the strength and courage to carry on.

Section 1 - Finding Joy Amidst Sorrow

This section contains chapters that focus on navigating the complexities of grief, composing a heartfelt eulogy, and cherishing the memories of the departed. It offers guidance on managing emotions, cultivating the right mindset for crafting and delivering the eulogy, and coping with the overwhelming wave of feelings that may arise.

While embarking on this emotional journey may be challenging, it can ultimately lead to healing and a sense of fulfillment as you pay tribute to your loved one and provide solace to those in mourning. By attaining a state of mental and emotional clarity, you can channel your thoughts and emotions constructively, despite the grief caused by the sudden loss of your beloved.

1. Celebrating The Life Of Someone Who Passed From Sudden Illness

1.1 Introduction: Reflecting On The Impact Of Sudden Illness On Our Lives

1.1.1 Understanding The Shock Of Sudden Illness

Sudden illness has a way of blindsiding us, catching us off guard and leaving us grappling with a whirlwind of emotions. It's like a plot twist in the movie of life that we never saw coming. We're left in a state of disbelief, questioning how something so unexpected could happen to someone we hold dear.

1.1.2 The Emotional Turmoil Of Sudden Loss

When someone we love passes away from a sudden illness, the emotional roller coaster we find ourselves on can be overwhelming. From disbelief to anger, from profound sadness to a feeling of emptiness, we experience a wide range of emotions. Navigating this emotional turmoil is a challenging journey that takes time and support from our loved ones.

1.2. Capturing The Essence: Celebrating The Unique Qualities And Memories Of The Departed

1.2.1 Highlighting Their Passions And Interests

One way to remember and honor the life of someone who passed from sudden illness is to celebrate the unique qualities that made them who they were. Whether it was their infectious love for gardening or their unwavering dedication to their favorite sports team, highlighting their passions and interests can help us cherish their individuality.

1.2.2 Recalling Special Moments Shared Together

We are fortunate to have a treasure trove of memories with our departed loved ones. From road trips that turned into unforgettable adventures to lazy afternoons filled with laughter and heartfelt conversations, these special moments are the threads that weave together the tapestry of our shared lives. Remembering these cherished moments can bring comfort and allow us to keep their spirit alive.

1.3. Honoring Their Legacy: Recognizing The Accomplishments And Contributions Of The Person

1.3.1 Exploring Their Professional Achievements And Impact

Many individuals who pass from sudden illness have made significant contributions in their professional lives. Whether they were trailblazers in their industry or made a difference in the lives of their colleagues, taking the time to recognize and celebrate their professional achievements can be a meaningful way to honor their legacy.

1.3.2 Recognizing Their Philanthropic Endeavors

Some people leave behind a legacy of giving back and making a positive impact on their community. Whether through volunteering, charitable donations, or advocating for important causes, their philanthropic endeavors deserve recognition and celebration. By acknowledging their efforts, we not only honor their memory but also inspire others to follow in their footsteps.

1.4. Embracing Joyful Remembrance: Finding Solace In Happy Memories And Cherished Moments

1.4.1 Treasuring Laughter And Shared Experiences

Laughter has a unique way of bringing people together and creating cherished memories. When remembering someone who passed from sudden illness, we should embrace the joy that they brought into our lives. Reminisce about the times you shared laughter and celebrate the happiness that they brought into your life.

1.4.2 Emphasizing The Importance Of Celebrating Their Life

While it's natural to mourn the loss of a loved one, it's equally important to celebrate their life. Reflecting on the joy they brought, the love they shared, and the impact they had can help us find solace amidst the sorrow. By celebrating their life, we ensure that their memory lives on and that their legacy continues to inspire and uplift others.

In the midst of our grief, it's essential to remember that celebrating the life of someone who passed from sudden illness can bring comfort, joy, and a sense of closure. By highlighting their unique qualities, treasuring shared memories, honoring their accomplishments, and embracing joyful remembrance, we ensure that their spirit lives on in our hearts.

1.5. Coming Together: Exploring The Importance Of Community And Support During Times Of Grief

1.5.1 Building A Support Network Through Family And Friends

When we face the loss of a loved one, it's important to remember that we don't have to go through it alone. Building a support network through family and friends can provide us with the comfort and strength we need during times of grief. Whether it's a shoulder to cry on, a listening ear, or simply someone to share memories with, having loved ones around can make all the difference. So reach out to those closest to you and let them be there for you in your time of need.

1.5.2 The Role Of Community In Providing Comfort And Solace

In times of sorrow, our community can become a source of immense comfort and solace. Attending support groups or seeking solace in religious or spiritual communities can offer a sense of belonging and understanding. Sharing stories, memories, and finding common ground with others who have experienced similar loss can help us navigate the complexities of grief. Communities have an incredible way of coming together and supporting each other, reminding us that we are not alone in our pain.

1.6. Rituals Of Remembrance: Exploring Meaningful Ways To Celebrate And Honor The Life Of The Departed

1.6.1 Organizing A Memorial Service Or Ceremony

One way to celebrate and honor the life of someone who has passed is by organizing a memorial service or ceremony. This can be a beautiful opportunity to bring together friends and family to remember and pay tribute to the departed. Whether it's a formal gathering or an intimate affair, the act of coming together to share stories, laughter, and tears can help us find solace and create lasting memories. It's a chance to reflect on the impact the person had on our lives and to celebrate the unique individual they were.

1.6.2 Creating Personalized Tributes And Keepsakes

Another meaningful way to honor the memory of someone dear is by creating personalized tributes and keepsakes. This could involve compiling a photo album or a collage of memories, writing a heartfelt letter, or even creating a piece of art inspired by their life. These personalized tributes offer a tangible reminder of the joy they brought into our lives and can be cherished for years to come. It's a way to keep their spirit alive and to celebrate the unique bond we shared.

1.7. Celebrating Life: Focusing On The Positive Aspects Of The Person's Journey And The Lessons Learned

1.7.1 Reflecting On Personal Growth And Resilience

In the midst of grief, it can be helpful to reflect on our own personal growth and resilience that we've gained through the presence of our departed loved one. We can celebrate the ways they contributed to our lives by acknowledging the positive impact they had on our personal development. Even in their absence, we can carry forward the lessons they taught us and the strength they instilled in us, finding solace in the growth that has come from knowing them.

1.7.2 Embracing The Lessons Taught By The Departed

The people who touch our lives often leave behind valuable lessons that deserve to be celebrated. Take the time to reflect on the lessons taught by the departed and how they have influenced and shaped you. Perhaps they taught you to be kinder, to embrace adventure, or to never give up. By embracing these lessons and incorporating them into our own lives, we can find comfort and a way to honor their memory. Celebrating their life means celebrating the wisdom they imparted to us.

1.8. Moving Forward With Hope: Finding Healing And Strength In The Midst Of Sorrow

1.8.1 Embracing The Grieving Process And Seeking Support

Moving forward after losing someone to sudden illness is a journey that takes time and patience. It's essential to embrace the grieving process and allow ourselves to feel the full range of emotions. Seeking support from friends, family, or even professional counselors can help us navigate through the pain and find healing. Remember, healing doesn't mean forgetting; it means learning to live with our loss and finding a way to honor the departed while finding our own strength to move forward.

1.8.2 Finding Hope And Purpose In Life After Loss

Although it may seem impossible at first, there is hope and purpose to be found in life after loss. As we navigate the grieving process, we discover a newfound appreciation for the fragility and preciousness of life. This awareness can inspire us to live more fully, to pursue our dreams, and to cherish each moment. By honoring the memory of our departed loved one and finding strength in their legacy, we can find hope in the darkness and begin to rebuild our lives with a renewed sense of purpose.

As we conclude this exploration of celebrating the life of someone who passed from sudden illness, let us remember that our loved ones would want us to find healing and strength. Though the pain may never fully disappear, we can choose to honor their memory by embracing joyful remembrance and cherishing the moments we shared. By coming together as a community, supporting one another, and finding solace in rituals of remembrance, we can navigate the journey of grief with resilience and hope. May the memories of our departed loved ones continue to bring us comfort and inspire us to live each day to the fullest.

2. Healing In Times Of Grief: Crafting A Meaningful Eulogy For A Sudden Illness Fatality

Grief is a deeply personal and complex emotion, particularly when we are faced with the sudden loss of a loved one to illness. In these challenging times, crafting a meaningful eulogy can be a powerful tool for healing and honoring the life of the departed. A eulogy offers us an opportunity to reflect on cherished memories, express our emotions, and find solace in shared experiences. This chapter explores the significance of a eulogy in the grieving process and provides guidance on how to create a personalized tribute that captures the essence of the individual, brings comfort to those in mourning, and helps us embrace healing as we navigate life after loss.

2.1. Understanding The Power Of A Eulogy In The Healing Process

2.1.1 The Role Of Eulogies In The Grieving Process

When we lose someone to sudden illness, it can feel like our world has been turned upside down. In times of grief, a eulogy can play a vital role in the healing process. It allows us to remember and honor the life of our loved one, while also providing a space to express our emotions and find solace in shared memories.

2.1.2 The Therapeutic Benefits Of Delivering A Eulogy

Delivering a eulogy may seem daunting, but it can also be incredibly therapeutic. It gives us the opportunity to not only pay tribute to the departed, but also to process our own feelings of grief and loss. Speaking about our loved one allows us to reflect on their impact on our lives and find closure in celebrating their legacy.

2.2. Honoring The Life And Legacy Of The Departed: Gathering Memories And Stories

2.2.1 Collecting Personal Stories And Memories

One of the most beautiful aspects of crafting a eulogy is gathering personal stories and memories from family and friends. These anecdotes offer a glimpse into the unique qualities and experiences that made the departed special. Whether it's recounting a funny incident or sharing a heartfelt moment, these stories help paint a vivid picture of their life and create a meaningful eulogy.

2.2.2 Interviewing Family And Friends To Capture Key Moments

To truly honor the life and legacy of the departed, it's important to interview family and friends who knew them well. By doing so, you can capture key moments and significant events that shaped their journey. These interviews provide valuable insights and help ensure that your eulogy captures the essence of the individual, showcasing their passions, achievements, and impact on others.

2.3. Unveiling The Emotional Journey: Expressing Grief, Love, And Loss

2.3.1 Reflecting On The Emotional Impact Of Sudden Illness

Losing someone to sudden illness can leave us grappling with a whirlwind of emotions. When crafting a eulogy, it's essential to reflect on the emotional impact this loss has had on us and others. By acknowledging our grief and the depth of our love for the departed, we create a space for healing and allow those in attendance to connect on a deeper level.

2.3.2 Articulating Feelings Of Grief And Loss

Expressing our feelings of grief and loss in a eulogy can be challenging but cathartic. It's important to find the right balance between honoring the departed and allowing ourselves to be vulnerable. By sharing our authentic emotions, we not only validate our own grief but also provide comfort to others who may be experiencing similar feelings. This shared experience can help foster a sense of unity and support during a difficult time.

2.4. Crafting A Personalized Eulogy: Capturing The Essence Of The Individual

2.4.1 Highlighting The Unique Qualities And Accomplishments

Every individual is unique, and a eulogy should reflect that. Highlighting the departed's unique qualities and accomplishments allows us to celebrate their individuality and the positive impact they made during their time with us. From their sense of humor to their dedication to their passions, it's important to showcase the aspects that made them truly special.

2.4.2 Incorporating Personal Anecdotes And Shared Experiences

Incorporating personal anecdotes and shared experiences into a eulogy ensures that it captures the essence of the departed. Whether it's a funny story that perfectly encapsulates their personality or a shared experience that symbolizes their values, these moments provide a heartfelt connection and make the eulogy feel personal and authentic. By sharing these anecdotes, we not only honor the departed but also allow others to reminisce and find comfort in these shared memories.

2.5. Finding Strength In Shared Experiences: Inviting Others To Participate

2.5.1 Encouraging Family And Friends To Share Their Stories

When it comes to crafting a meaningful eulogy for someone who has been lost to sudden illness, one of the most powerful ways to honor their memory is by inviting family and friends to share their stories. These personal anecdotes provide comfort and serve as a reminder of the impact their loved one had on those around them. Encourage those close to the deceased to reflect on their experiences and share their fondest memories. This not only adds depth and richness to the eulogy but also allows everyone to find solace in the shared connection and collective grieving process.

2.5.2 Collaborating On The Eulogy With Loved Ones

The task of crafting a eulogy can seem daunting, especially when faced with the weight of grief. However, it doesn't have to be a burden borne by one person alone. Consider collaborating with other loved ones to create a collective tribute that truly captures the essence of the person being honored. By sharing the responsibility of creating the eulogy, you not only lighten the load but also gain diverse perspectives and insights that may have otherwise been missed. Working together ensures that the eulogy reflects the collective voice and memories of those who held the deceased dear, making it a more comprehensive and meaningful tribute.

2.6. Providing Comfort And Solace: Addressing The Pain And Offering Hope

2.6.1 Acknowledging The Pain And Difficulties Of Grief

Grief is a complex and challenging journey, particularly when someone we love is taken away by sudden illness. It is important to acknowledge and address the pain and difficulties that accompany the grieving process in the eulogy. By acknowledging the range of emotions, from profound sadness to anger to confusion, we validate the experiences of those in mourning. Sharing these sentiments also allows others to feel seen and understood, providing a sense of comfort in knowing that their grief is not isolated or unnatural.

2.6.2 Offering Words Of Comfort, Hope, And Healing

Amidst the pain, it is vital to offer words of comfort, hope, and healing in the eulogy. Weaving in heartfelt words that provide solace can help alleviate some of the burden carried by grieving hearts. Share kind thoughts, gentle reminders of love, and messages of hope for the future.

Emphasize the resilience of the human spirit and the capacity to heal over time. By offering words that uplift and inspire, the eulogy becomes a source of strength for those in mourning, reminding them that they are not alone and that healing is possible.

2.7. Healing Through Rituals And Symbolism: Creating A Meaningful Ceremony

2.7.1 Incorporating Rituals And Symbolic Gestures In The Eulogy

Rituals and symbolic gestures have long been used to honor the departed and create a sense of closure. Consider incorporating meaningful rituals or symbolic gestures into the eulogy itself. This could be as simple as lighting a candle or sharing a moment of silence to commemorate the deceased. By infusing the eulogy with these rituals, you establish a sense of reverence and create a space for healing and reflection.

2.7.2 Creating A Sacred Space For Healing And Reflection

In addition to incorporating rituals and symbolism into the eulogy, creating a sacred space for healing and reflection can profoundly impact the grieving process. Choose a location, whether it be a place of worship, a serene outdoor setting, or a personal space that holds significance, to host the ceremony. Pay attention to the atmosphere, ensuring it fosters a sense of peace and tranquility. By intentionally curating the environment, the eulogy becomes part of a larger healing experience, encouraging attendees to find solace and reflect on their own journey of healing.

2.8. Moving Forward With Resilience: Embracing Life After Loss

2.8.1 Finding Strength In The Process Of Healing

As challenging as it may seem, finding strength in the process of healing is a vital part of moving forward after loss. The eulogy can serve as a reminder that healing is not a linear path but a journey of ups and downs. Share stories of resilience and the ways in which the deceased faced adversity, highlighting their ability to navigate through difficult times. By illustrating these instances, the eulogy becomes an inspiration for those in mourning, providing hope that they too possess the strength to rebuild their lives despite the pain.

2.8.2 Nurturing Resilience And Continuing The Legacy

When crafting the eulogy, consider how to nurture resilience and honor the legacy of the departed. Encourage those in mourning to find ways to carry forward the lessons, values, and passions of their loved one. Emphasize the importance of embracing life and continuing the impact they had on the world. By nurturing resilience and honoring the legacy in the eulogy, you give mourners a sense of purpose and a roadmap for navigating life after loss.

As we conclude this journey of embracing healing in times of grief, remember that crafting a meaningful eulogy is a profound act of love and remembrance. By gathering memories, expressing emotions, and finding strength in shared experiences, we can create a powerful tribute that not only honors the life and legacy of the departed but also provides comfort and solace to ourselves and others. May the process of writing and delivering a eulogy serve as a transformative experience, helping us navigate the path of healing and resilience as we move forward with cherished memories and a renewed appreciation for life.

3. Farewell To A Dear Friend: Sharing Memories And Saying Goodbye

3.1. Introduction: A Reflection On The Importance Of Farewell

3.1.1 The Role Of Farewell In The Grieving Process

Saying goodbye can be one of the most challenging aspects of losing a dear friend. Yet, it is also an essential part of the grieving process. Farewell allows us to acknowledge the reality of their absence and begin to come to terms with our loss. It provides closure and allows us to move forward in our own journeys of healing.

3.1.2 Acknowledging The Significance Of Saying Goodbye

While bidding farewell may feel painful, it holds great significance. It is a way for us to honor our friendship and the value that our departed friend brought to our lives. Saying goodbye allows us to express our love, gratitude, and appreciation for the moments we shared together. It is an opportunity to reflect on the impact they had and the legacy they leave behind.

3.2. Cherishing Memories: Recounting The Shared Experiences

3.2.1 Reminiscing The Fond Memories Together

In times of loss, memories become treasures that we hold close to our hearts. Take the time to reminisce about the cherished moments you had with your friend. Recall the laughter, the adventures, and the deep conversations. Allow yourself to feel the joy and warmth that those memories bring. Sharing these recollections with others who knew and loved your friend can bring solace and help keep their spirit alive.

3.2.2 Sharing Anecdotes And Stories

Funny, heartwarming, or even slightly embarrassing anecdotes and stories are the threads that weave the tapestry of friendship. By sharing these stories, we not only keep our friend's memory alive but also create a sense of connection and unity among those who gather to say goodbye. Let the laughter and tears flow as you reminisce and celebrate the unique experiences and adventures you had together.

3.3. Celebrating Their Life: Honoring Achievements And Impact

3.3.1 Recognizing Their Accomplishments And Contributions

Our departed friends leave behind a legacy of their accomplishments and contributions. As we bid them farewell, it is important to take a moment to recognize and celebrate these achievements. Whether it's their professional milestones, personal triumphs, or acts of kindness, honoring their accomplishments helps us appreciate the fullness of their life and the impact they made on others.

3.3.2 Highlighting Their Positive Influence On Others

A dear friend often has a way of impacting the lives of those around them. They inspire, support, and uplift us during both the good and challenging times. Take the opportunity to shine a light on the positive influence your friend had on others. Share stories of how they made a difference, touched hearts, and left an indelible mark on the lives they touched. In doing so, their impact continues to live on and inspire others.

3.4. Gathering Loved Ones: Planning A Farewell Ceremony

3.4.1 Choosing A Suitable Venue For The Ceremony

When planning a farewell ceremony, consider selecting a venue that holds significance for both your departed friend and the people attending. It could be a place they loved, a location tied to precious memories, or a setting that reflects their personality. Choosing a meaningful venue can create a comforting and intimate atmosphere for everyone to gather, remember, and support one another.

3.4.2 Organizing Logistics And Invitations

Organizing a farewell ceremony involves handling logistical aspects such as scheduling, invitations, and any necessary arrangements. Reach out to friends and family, ensuring that no one who wishes to attend is overlooked. It can be helpful to assign tasks to different individuals who are willing to contribute. Remember, planning a farewell is not a burden to bear alone; by involving loved ones, you can create a collective effort of love and support.

3.5. Expressing Grief: Coping With Loss And Emotions

3.5.1 Understanding The Different Stages Of Grief

Losing a dear friend is never easy. It's important to remember that grief is a natural response to loss, and it often comes in waves. You may find yourself experiencing a range of emotions, from sadness and anger to confusion and even relief. These emotions may not always follow a linear path, and that's okay. Understanding the different stages of grief, such as denial, anger, bargaining, depression, and acceptance, can help you navigate through the rollercoaster of emotions. Just remember, there is no "right" or "wrong" way to grieve.

3.5.2 Finding Healthy Ways To Process And Express Emotions

Processing your emotions is an important part of healing. Find healthy outlets to express yourself: write in a journal, engage in physical activities like walking or yoga, or talk to a trusted friend or therapist. Don't be afraid to cry or laugh, as both can be cathartic. Remember that grief is a personal journey, so allow yourself the time and space to feel and grieve in your own unique way.

3.6. The Healing Power Of Rituals: Creating Meaningful Farewell Traditions

3.6.1 Exploring Rituals And Ceremonies From Different Cultures

Rituals play a significant role in saying goodbye and honoring the departed. Take the time to explore different cultural traditions and rituals surrounding death and mourning. Whether it's lighting candles, releasing lanterns, or holding a memorial service, these customs can provide a sense of comfort and closure. Borrow from various traditions, adapt them to your own beliefs, or create new rituals that resonate with your friend's life and spirit. Most importantly, it is crucial to show respect for the beliefs of others, particularly those who are mourning the loss of a loved one.

3.6.2 Designing Personalized Rituals To Honor The Departed

Personalizing rituals can make them even more meaningful. Think about what made your friendship special and how you can incorporate those elements into a farewell ceremony. Consider creating a memory board filled with photos, sharing stories and anecdotes during a gathering, or planting a tree in their honor. By designing personalized rituals, you not only pay tribute to your dear friend but also create a space for healing and reminiscing.

3.7. Supporting Each Other: Navigating The Grieving Process Together

3.7.1 Forming A Support System And Seeking Help

Grieving is not something you have to do alone. Reach out to others who are also mourning the loss and form a support system. Sharing your feelings and memories can provide solace and comfort. Additionally, don't hesitate to seek professional help if needed. Therapists and support groups can offer guidance and provide a safe space to process your emotions. Remember, it is okay to ask for help and take care of yourself during this time of mourning.

3.7.2 Providing Comfort And Understanding To Others

Supporting others through their grief is just as important as receiving support yourself. It is a reciprocal relationship, where giving and receiving support go hand in hand. Be there for your friends, family, and others who are mourning. Offer a listening ear, a shoulder to cry on, or a simple gesture of kindness. By being there for others in their time of need, you are not only providing comfort but also creating a sense of community and connection. Remember, different people grieve in different ways, so be patient and understanding. Your compassion can make a world of difference during this challenging time.

3.8. Embracing The Legacy: Carrying Forward The Memories And Lessons Learned

3.8.1 Preserving The Memory Of The Departed Through Keepsakes

While our dear friend may no longer be physically present, their memory can live on through keepsakes. Create a memory box filled with mementos, letters, and photos that remind you of the good times you shared. You can also consider creating a tribute video or compiling a scrapbook to honor their life. By preserving their memory, you keep their spirit alive and ensure that their impact on your life is never forgotten.

3.8.2 Applying The Lessons Learned From Their Life In Our Own

Drawing inspiration from the life of our dear friends can be a powerful way to honor their memory and find meaning in their departure. Reflecting on the qualities they possessed, the values they held dear, and the lessons they taught can guide us in our own lives. Whether it be kindness, resilience, or the pursuit of passions, incorporating these lessons into our daily routines can help us carry forward their legacy.

As we reach the end of this chapter in the heartfelt journey of bidding farewell, let us remember that saying goodbye signifies not just an end, but a fresh start. By reminiscing about shared memories, acknowledging accomplishments, and embracing traditions, we find solace in the therapeutic nature of recollection. Let us continue to offer each other support, recognizing the lasting impact our beloved friends have had on us.

May their legacy serve as a source of inspiration for us to live life to the fullest, love unconditionally, and cherish the moments we share with those we hold close to our hearts. Let us find comfort in knowing that their spirit lives on in the love and laughter we continue to share with others. And as we bid our final adieu, let us always keep their memory alive within us.

4. The Power Of Memories: Honoring Someone Lost To Sudden Illness Through Words

4.1. Introduction: The Significance Of Memories In Honoring Those Lost To Sudden Illness

Grief is a deeply personal and challenging journey, particularly when it comes to the sudden loss of a loved one due to illness. In these heartbreaking moments, memories become powerful tools for honoring and cherishing the lives of those we have lost. Memories hold the essence of individuals, encapsulating their unique personalities, experiences, and impact on our lives. This chapter explores the profound significance of memories in the grieving process, offering insights into how to navigate the complexities of sudden illness, preserve cherished moments, and find solace through the healing power of words. By sharing stories and embracing memories, we can honor the lives of those we have lost and find strength in their lasting legacy.

4.1.1 The Lasting Impact Of Sudden Illness

Sudden illness can turn our lives upside down in an instant. The shock and grief that comes with losing someone unexpectedly can leave us feeling lost and overwhelmed. Each person's experience is unique, but one thing remains constant: the lasting impact it has on our lives and our memories.

4.1.2 The Role Of Memories In The Grieving Process

Memories are powerful, serving as a bridge between the past and the present. When we lose someone to sudden illness, memories become even more significant. They allow us to celebrate and honor the life that was, to cherish the moments we shared, and to keep their spirit alive within us. Memories become our way of coping and healing.

4.2. Understanding The Impact Of Sudden Illness: Coping With Unexpected Loss

4.2.1 The Shock And Trauma Of Sudden Illness

Sudden illness often strikes without warning, leaving us in a state of shock and disbelief. The unexpected nature of the loss can make it difficult to process our emotions, leaving us feeling overwhelmed and unsure of how to move forward. The initial shock and trauma take time to navigate as we come to terms with the reality of our loved one's absence.

4.2.2 Navigating The Stages Of Grief

The stages of grief, including denial, anger, bargaining, depression, and acceptance, are well-known but can feel like a tumultuous roller coaster ride. Navigating through these stages is a personal journey, and it's important to remember that there is no set timeline for grief. Each person will experience it in their own way, and memories play a crucial role in helping us process and navigate these stages.

4.3. The Healing Power Of Words: Exploring The Role Of Memories In The Grieving Process

4.3.1 Expressing Emotions Through Writing

Writing provides an outlet for our emotions during the grieving process. It allows us to express our deepest sorrows, joys, and love that we still hold for the person we lost. Through words, we can paint a picture of who they were and how they impacted our lives. Writing gives us the space to release our pent-up emotions and find solace in the memories we hold dear.

4.3.2 Connecting With Memories As A Source Of Comfort And Healing

Memories have an incredible power to bring comfort and healing during times of grief. They allow us to relive moments of happiness, laughter, and love shared with our loved one. By reconnecting with these memories, we remind ourselves that their presence, though physically gone, continues to live on in our hearts. Memories become a source of solace, reminding us that while they may be absent from our lives, they will never be forgotten.

4.4. Preserving Memories: Strategies For Capturing And Preserving Cherished Moments

4.4.1 Importance Of Documenting Memories

Documenting memories becomes essential in honoring those we've lost to sudden illness. Whether it's through writing, photography, or other forms of creative expression, capturing these cherished moments ensures that they remain alive and tangible. By documenting our memories, we create a lasting tribute to their impact on our lives and provide future generations with a window into the beautiful soul we were fortunate to know.

4.4.2 Utilizing Different Mediums To Preserve Memories

In this digital age, we have numerous mediums at our disposal to preserve memories. From creating a scrapbook or a memory box filled with mementos to creating online photo albums or dedicating a blog or social media page to our loved one's memory, the possibilities are endless. By utilizing these different mediums, we can ensure that the memories we hold dear are preserved in a way that feels personal and meaningful to us.

Remember, honoring someone lost to sudden illness through words is a testament to their impact on our lives. It allows us to find comfort, healing, and a sense of connection even in their physical absence. The power of memories is immeasurable; they remind us that love transcends time and that the ones we hold dear will forever remain a part of us.

4.5. Crafting A Tribute: Writing Heartfelt Words To Honor The Memory Of A Loved One

Losing a loved one to sudden illness is an indescribable pain that leaves a void in our lives. One way to honor their memory is by crafting a heartfelt tribute that captures the essence of their life and the impact they had on those around them. While writing about someone you've lost can be challenging, it can also be a cathartic and healing process.

4.5.1 Reflecting On The Impact Of The Lost Loved One

Before you begin writing, take some time to reflect on the impact your loved one had on your life and the lives of others. Think about their unique qualities, their passions, and the memories you shared together. Remember the moments that made you smile, the lessons they taught you, and the ways in which they touched the hearts of those around them. As you begin to put pen to paper, let the memories of your loved one guide your words. Share the stories that made them unique, the moments that brought laughter and tears, and the legacy they left behind. Remember that through your eulogy, you have the power to honor their life and keep their spirit alive in the hearts of those who hear your words.

4.5.2 Tips For Writing A Meaningful Tribute

- Be authentic: Write from the heart and don't worry about being overly formal or eloquent. The most meaningful tributes are those that are genuine and heartfelt.

- Share anecdotes: Highlight specific moments or stories that encapsulate the essence of your loved one. These personal anecdotes can bring their spirit to life and create a deeper connection with readers.

- Focus on their positive qualities: While it's important to acknowledge the pain of loss, also highlight the positive qualities, achievements, and the love they brought into the world. This can become a source of comfort and inspiration for others.

- Use humor if appropriate: Remember that life isn't always serious, and adding a touch of humor can reflect the personality of your loved one and bring warmth to the tribute.

- Edit and revise: After drafting your tribute, give it some time and then come back to it with fresh eyes. Edit and revise as needed to ensure you've captured the essence of your loved one.

4.6. Sharing Memories: Creating A Supportive Community Within The Grieving Process

Grief can often feel isolating, but sharing memories of our loved ones can create a supportive community that understands and empathizes with our pain. Creating a space where people can come together to share stories and memories can be incredibly healing.

4.6.1 Establishing A Safe Space To Share Memories

Whether it's through a private online platform, a memorial event, or a simple gathering with close friends and family, establishing a safe space to share memories can be cathartic. Encourage others to participate by sharing their own stories and experiences, creating a supportive environment where people feel comfortable expressing their grief.

4.6.2 The Importance Of Empathy And Active Listening

In these shared spaces, it's crucial to practice empathy and active listening. Everyone grieves differently, and it's important to validate and respect each individual's experience. Focus on being present, offering understanding and support to those who choose to open up. Sometimes, the simple act of listening can provide immense comfort to someone in the midst of their grief.

4.7. Finding Solace Through Storytelling: The Therapeutic Benefits Of Sharing Personal Experiences

Sharing personal stories and experiences not only creates a supportive community but also offers therapeutic benefits for both the storyteller and the listener. By sharing our own journeys, we can find solace and help others going through similar experiences.

4.7.1 Healing Through Narrative

Storytelling allows us to process our emotions, unravel our thoughts, and find meaning in the face of loss. As we recount our memories and experiences, we begin to understand ourselves and our grief on a deeper level. Through narrative, we can find healing and make sense of the complex emotions that come with losing someone suddenly.

4.7.2 Encouraging Others To Share Their Own Stories

Encouraging others to share their own stories not only provides them with an outlet, but it also allows for a deeper connection within the grieving community. By fostering an environment that encourages storytelling, we create a space where individuals can find support, strength, and understanding in their shared experiences.

4.8. Moving Forward: Embracing Memories As A Source Of Strength And Inspiration

While the pain of losing someone suddenly never completely fades, embracing memories can help us find strength and inspiration as we navigate life without our loved ones.

4.8.1 Transforming Grief Into Resilience

Memories have the power to transform grief into resilience. By reminiscing about the love, joy, and lessons our loved ones brought into our lives, we can draw strength during difficult times. Embracing their memory allows their spirit to live on within us, providing us with the resilience needed to face the challenges that lie ahead.

4.8.2 The Legacy Of Memories In Shaping The Future

The memories we hold dear become a unique legacy that shapes not only our individual lives but also the lives of those around us. By cherishing the memories of our lost loved ones, we can keep their legacies alive and carry their influence into the future. Our memories become a guiding light, inspiring us to live fully and embrace the precious moments life has to offer.

As we navigate the painful journey of grieving a loved one lost to sudden illness, we must remember that memories can serve as a source of solace, healing, and inspiration. By capturing and preserving cherished moments, crafting heartfelt tributes, and sharing our stories, we create a supportive community that honors the lives of those we have lost. In embracing memories, we find the strength to move forward, transforming grief into resilience. Let us hold onto the power of memories, allowing them to guide us as we navigate the path of healing and keep the spirit of our loved ones alive.

Section 2 - Eulogy Templates And Sections

The upcoming chapters feature three eulogies that are carefully structured to honor those who have passed away unexpectedly due to illness. These eulogies are divided into specific sections that are designed to help you create a heartfelt tribute to your loved ones. You are free to choose which sections to include based on your personal preferences and circumstances. Add quotes and anecdotes about the deceased to any of the relevant sections to capture their unique journey and impact on others. Be empowered to make any edits or additions that resonate with your own experiences.

Furthermore, you have the flexibility to mix and match sections from the different eulogies to craft a truly unique, personalized and fitting tribute. Alternatively, you can use these eulogies as a source of inspiration to create your own original eulogy.

May you find this section to be a valuable source of guidance during this difficult time and may you find solace and strength to endure.

5. Eulogy 1 - Farewell To An Angel Taken Too Soon

5.1 Introduction And Setting The Tone

Ladies and Gentlemen,

In this heartfelt tribute, we gather to honor and remember the extraordinary life of [Name]. [Name]'s presence touched the lives of many, leaving an indelible mark that transcends time. I am [Your Name], [Name/s]'s [Your relationship to the deceased] and I am honored to speak on behalf of the loved ones gathered. As we come together to celebrate their life, we reflect on the profound impact [Name] had on both the [community/industry/field] and the lives of their loved ones. Through their unwavering passion, remarkable achievements, and enduring legacy, [Name] continues to inspire and uplift us, even in their absence. Join us on this journey as we pay tribute to an angel taken too soon.

5.1.1 The Loved Ones And Legacy

Our beloved [Name/s] has/have passed away, leaving a void in our lives. [Name/s] is/are survived by [his/her/their] loving family, including [his/her/their] devoted [husband/wife/spouse],

[Name] and their [number] children [List Names]. [He/She/They] also leave behind cherished relatives, nieces, nephews, and cousins. [Name/s] touched the lives of many friends and acquaintances with [his/her/their] graciousness and support. [He/She/They] will be greatly missed but [his/her/their] impact on those [he/she/they] touched remains.

[**Prompt:** Adjust this section as necessary to include family, relatives, friends and other close or notable acquaintances.]

5.2 Remembering The Life

5.2.1 Early Life And Background

In this bittersweet tribute, we gather to remember the life and legacy of [Name], an angel taken from us far too soon. From the very beginning, it was evident that [Name] possessed a spark that set them apart. Born and raised in [hometown], [Name] had a humble and down-to-earth upbringing that shaped their character and values.

5.2.2 Passion And Dreams

[Name]'s passion for [field/industry] was unparalleled. From a young age, they knew exactly what they wanted to contribute to this world.

[Name]'s dreams and ambitions were as vast as the universe, and they pursued them relentlessly. Their unwavering determination and drive served as a beacon of inspiration for all who knew them.

5.2.3 Impact On Loved Ones

[Name] had an extraordinary ability to touch the lives of everyone they encountered. Their infectious laughter and genuine kindness were just a couple of the qualities that endeared them to others. [Name] had an uncanny way of making people feel seen and loved, leaving an indelible mark on the hearts of their loved ones. The void left by [Name]'s absence is immeasurable, but the memories of their love and warmth will continue to bring comfort to those who hold them dear.

5.3 Impact On The [Community/Industry/Field]

5.3.1 Breakthrough Achievements

In the [community/industry/field], [Name] made waves with their groundbreaking achievements. Their innovative ideas and unique perspective challenged the status quo and paved the way for new possibilities. [Name]'s impact and contributions transcended expectations, leaving an indelible imprint on the [community/industry/field] that will endure for generations to come.

5.3.2 Inspiring Change

[Name] was not one to sit idly by and accept the world as it was. They possessed an unwavering commitment to making a difference and inspiring change. Whether it was through their advocacy work, philanthropic endeavors, or contagious spirit, [Name] exemplified the power of one person to make a lasting impact and create a ripple effect of positive change.

5.3.3 Influence On Others

[Name]'s influence extended far beyond their immediate circle. They had an innate ability to inspire and motivate others to discover their own potential. Many credit [Name] as the catalyst that propelled them to chase their dreams and overcome obstacles. Their legacy lives on through the countless lives they touched, forever imprinted with their courage and unwavering belief in the human spirit.

5.4 Personal Stories And Memories

5.4.1 Fond Memories Shared By Family And Friends

As we reflect on [Name]'s life, memories of warmth and laughter flood our hearts. [Name] had an uncanny ability to bring people together, creating lifelong bonds and fostering a sense of belonging. Friends and family recount stories of shared adventures, inside jokes, and cherished moments that will forever be etched in their minds.

5.4.2 Touching Moments With [Name]

It was in [Name]'s presence that magical moments seemed to unfold. Their ability to find joy in the simplest of things and their genuine interest in the lives of others made every interaction with them feel like a gift. From impromptu dance parties to heartfelt conversations under the stars, [Name] had a way of making ordinary moments extraordinary.

5.4.3 Lessons Learned from [Name]

[Name]'s legacy extends beyond their accomplishments. They taught us invaluable lessons in love, resilience, and embracing life to the fullest. Through their unwavering spirit and determination, [Name] showed us the importance of pursuing our passions wholeheartedly, cherishing our relationships, and living each day with purpose.

5.5 Contributions And Achievements

5.5.1 Notable Accomplishments

[Name] leaves behind an impressive array of accomplishments that serve as a testament to their talent and dedication. From [specific achievement] to [notable milestone], [Name] consistently pushed boundaries and achieved greatness. Their tenacity and unwavering commitment to their craft set them apart as a true trailblazer.

5.5.2 Awards And Recognitions

Throughout their remarkable journey, [Name] received well-deserved recognition for their exceptional contributions. Their talent and impact were acknowledged with prestigious awards such as [specific awards]. These accolades not only validated [Name]'s brilliance but also inspired others to strive for excellence in their own endeavors.

5.5.3 Impactful Projects And Initiatives

[Name]'s legacy is alive in the projects and initiatives they spearheaded. From [example project/initiative] to [another project/initiative], [Name] poured their heart and soul into making a lasting difference in [relevant field/industry]. Their vision and dedication continue to shape the landscape of [field/industry], ensuring that the impact of their work endures long after their untimely departure.

5.6 Legacy And Influence: Work That Continues To Inspire

5.6.1 Continuing The Mission

Even though [Name] may no longer be with us, their mission and vision live on. Their work touched the lives of many, and it is up to us to carry the torch and continue their important work. Whether it was advocating for a cause, promoting creativity, or spreading kindness, we can honor [Name]'s memory by actively working towards the same goals. Let's keep the spirit of [Name]'s mission alive and make a difference in our own unique ways.

5.6.2 Individuals And Organizations Inspired

[Name] had a remarkable ability to inspire others. Countless individuals and organizations have been profoundly influenced by their life and work. From artists finding their creative voice to activists fighting for justice, [Name]'s impact can be seen in various fields. People are drawing strength and motivation from [Name]'s example and using it as fuel to make their own mark on the world. Their legacy lives on through the actions of those they inspired.

5.6.3 An Enduring Legacy

Some people leave footprints in the sand, but [Name] left an indelible mark on the world. Their legacy is one of compassion, passion, and making a difference. [Name]'s contributions will continue to shape the way we think, live, and interact with one another. Their ideas and values will remain influential and timeless, reminding us all of the importance of pursuing our passions and leaving the world a better place than we found it.

5.7 A Life Cut Short: Understanding The Loss

5.7.1 Tragic Circumstances Surrounding The Passing

The loss of [Name] is a heartbreaking tragedy. Their passing occurred under circumstances that have left us all reeling with shock and disbelief. It serves as a stark reminder of the fragility of life and the unpredictability of fate. We mourn the loss of someone who had so much more to give and achieve, leaving a void that can never be completely filled.

5.7.2 Impact On The Community

The impact [Name] had on the community cannot be overstated. Their presence brought joy, inspiration, and unity to those around them. Their absence is felt deeply by all who had the privilege of knowing them or experiencing their work. The community has come together to support one another during this difficult time, sharing stories, memories, and finding solace in the collective grief.

5.7.3 Coping With Grief And Loss

Losing someone as special as [Name] is incredibly painful, and it is essential to allow ourselves to grieve and process our emotions. While everyone copes with loss differently, it can be helpful to find support in loved ones, seek professional help if needed, and engage in self-care activities. Remember that it's okay to not have all the answers or to feel overwhelmed. Grief takes time, and healing is a personal journey.

5.8 Honoring The Memory: Memorial Services And Events

5.8.1 Funeral Arrangements And Tributes

In memory of [Name], funeral arrangements have been made to celebrate their life and provide an opportunity for family, friends, and admirers to say their goodbyes. The service will be a time to reflect on their legacy, share stories, and offer support to one another. Additionally, tributes and eulogies will be given to honor [Name]'s accomplishments and the impact they had on those around them.

5.8.2 Commemorative Events And Gatherings

Beyond the funeral, various commemorative events and gatherings are being organized. These events aim to bring together individuals who were touched by [Name]'s life and work. They will provide a space for people to share their memories, celebrate [Name]'s achievements, and find comfort in being surrounded by others who understand the depth of the loss.

5.8.3 Charitable Contributions In [Name]'s Honor

To honor [Name]'s memory and continue their philanthropic spirit, charitable contributions in their name are being accepted. These contributions will go towards causes and organizations that [Name] deeply cared about. By supporting these initiatives, we can make a difference in the areas that [Name] held close to their heart, creating a lasting testament to their values and the impact they had on the world.

5.9. Conclusion A: Celebrating The Life And Legacy

Although [Name] may have been taken from us far too soon, we can find solace in celebrating their life and the incredible legacy they've left behind. As we come together to mourn the loss, let's remember the joy, inspiration, and love that [Name] brought into our lives. Their memory will forever serve as a reminder to live passionately, make a positive impact, and cherish the moments we have with those we hold dear. Farewell, [Name], you will be missed, but never forgotten.

5.9. Conclusion B: Celebrating The Life And Legacy

As we draw this tribute to a close, we are reminded that although [Name] may no longer be physically present, their spirit lives on in the hearts and minds of those they touched. Through their contributions, achievements, and the memories shared by family and friends, [Name] has left an indelible legacy that will continue to inspire generations to come. Let us carry forward [Name]'s vision and passion, honoring their life by striving for greatness and making a positive impact in our own lives and communities. Farewell to our beloved [Name], an angel taken too soon, but whose light will forever shine brightly in our hearts.

6. Eulogy 2 - Reflecting On Life's Fragility, Embracing Hope: A Eulogy For Someone Lost Suddenly

6.1 Introduction A: Remembering A Life Lost Suddenly

Honored Guests,

In the face of sudden loss, our hearts are heavy with grief and our minds filled with questions. This eulogy serves as a tribute to someone who departed this world unexpectedly. It is a reflection on both the fragility of life and the enduring power of hope. I am [Your Name], [Name/s]'s [Your relationship to the deceased] and I am honored to speak on behalf of the loved ones gathered. Through shared stories, memories, and contemplation, we aim to honor the life and legacy of [Name], while also finding solace, strength, and inspiration in the face of such profound loss. Join us as we navigate the complexities of grief, celebrate the impact [Name] had on our lives, and embrace the hope that carries us forward.

6.1.1 The Shock Of Sudden Loss

Life has a way of throwing curveballs when we least expect them. The sudden loss of a loved one is a devastating blow that can leave us feeling disoriented and overwhelmed. It's as if the ground beneath our feet has been ripped away, leaving us grasping for stability in the midst of an emotional earthquake.

6.1.2 Reflecting On The Impact Of A Life Cut Short

When someone's life is cut short unexpectedly, it forces us to confront the fragility of our own existence. We are reminded that life is a precious gift, and we must cherish every moment we have with our loved ones. The sudden departure of someone dear to our hearts leaves us with a profound sense of loss, not just for the future experiences we will never share, but also for the memories that were never made.

6.1.3 The Loved Ones And Legacy

Our beloved [Name/s] has/have passed away, leaving a void in our lives. [Name] is survived by [his/her/their] loving family, including [his/her/their] devoted [husband/wife/spouse], [Name] and their [number] children [List Names]. [He/She/They] also leave behind cherished relatives, nieces, nephews, and cousins. [Name] touched the lives of many friends and acquaintances with [his/her/their] graciousness and support. [He/She/They] will be greatly missed but [his/her/their] impact on those [he/she/they] touched remains.

[**Prompt:** Adjust this section as necessary to include family, relatives, friends and other close or notable acquaintances.]

6.2 Celebrating The Life And Accomplishments

6.2.1 A Brief Overview Of [Name]'s Life And Achievements

In remembering [Name]'s life, we find solace in celebrating their accomplishments and the impact they made on those around them. [Name] lived a life filled with passion, determination, and a zest for making a difference. From their remarkable professional achievements to their acts of kindness and generosity, [Name] left an indelible mark on the world around them.

6.2.2 Fond Memories And Shared Experiences

As we gather here today, we bring with us a treasure trove of shared memories and experiences. From the memorable adventures to the heartfelt conversations, [Name] touched our lives in ways that cannot be easily forgotten. Whether it was their infectious laughter or their unwavering support during difficult times, [Name] had a unique ability to bring joy and comfort to those around them.

6.3. Embracing The Fragility Of Life: Reflections On Mortality

6.3.1 Contemplating The Transience Of Life

Losing someone suddenly forces us to confront our own mortality. It reminds us that life is a fleeting experience, and every breath we take is a reminder of its impermanence. It's a sobering thought, but one that can also serve as a catalyst for appreciating the beauty and preciousness of every moment we have.

6.3.2 Embracing The Impermanence And Uncertainty

In the face of uncertainty, we are presented with an opportunity to embrace life fully. Instead of fearing the unknown, we can choose to live with a sense of purpose and gratitude, cherishing every relationship, every experience, and every chance to make a positive impact. Life may be fragile, but it is also resilient, and it is up to us to make the most of the time we have.

6.4. Finding Strength In The Midst Of Grief: Coping With Sudden Loss

6.4.1 Navigating The Waves Of Grief

Grief comes in waves, crashing over us unexpectedly and leaving us breathless. It's important to remember that it's okay to feel a range of emotions during this time – sadness, anger, confusion, and even moments of laughter as we recall fond memories. We must allow ourselves the space to grieve and heal, understanding that there is no right or wrong way to mourn the loss of someone dear.

6.4.2 Seeking Support: Friends, Family, And Community

During times of profound loss, we often find strength in leaning on the support of others. Friends, family, and our wider community can provide a lifeline of comfort and understanding. Sharing our stories, seeking solace in shared experiences, and offering a listening ear can help ease the burden of grief. Together, we can navigate this difficult journey, finding solace in the knowledge that we are not alone.

Remember, in the midst of sorrow, there is always hope. Though we may grapple with the pain of loss, we can find solace in the memories we hold dear and the love that continues to flow through our veins. Let us honor the life that was lost suddenly by embracing the fragility of our own existence and living each day with purpose, kindness, and a heart full of love.

6.5 Honoring The Impact On Others: Stories Of Inspiration And Love

6.5.1 Touching Lives: Stories from The Inner Circle

As we gather here to remember and honor the life of our dear [Name], we are reminded of the profound impact they had on those closest to them. [Name] was a beacon of light, always ready with a kind word, a warm embrace, or a listening ear. Their friends and family have countless stories of the ways [Name] touched their lives, leaving an indelible mark of inspiration and love.

Perhaps it was the way [Name] would effortlessly make everyone feel included and appreciated. They had a knack for finding the good in people and bringing out the best in them. [Name]'s infectious laughter and genuine interest in others made every interaction with them feel like a gift.

There are stories of [Name] going above and beyond to help friends through tough times, offering unwavering support and encouragement. They were the rock that many leaned on during moments of uncertainty or despair. [Name]'s love and compassion had a remarkable way of healing hearts and giving hope.

6.5.2 Influence On The Wider Community

[Name]'s impact reached far beyond their immediate circle of loved ones. They passionately dedicated themselves to making a difference in the wider community, leaving an undeniable imprint on the lives of countless individuals.

Whether it was volunteering at local shelters, organizing fundraising events, or championing causes close to their heart, [Name] was committed to creating positive change. Their energy and enthusiasm were contagious, inspiring others to join in their mission and make a difference themselves.

[Name]'s legacy extends to the lives they touched through their work, their community involvement, and their unwavering belief in the power of kindness. Their memory will continue to inspire and guide us as we strive to follow in their footsteps, making the world a better place one act of love at a time.

6.6 Embracing Hope: Moving Forward And Finding Meaning In Loss

6.6.1 Finding Solace In Memories And Shared Values

While the pain of losing [Name] will always be present in our hearts, we can find solace in the memories we shared and the values they held dear. [Name] cherished family and friendship above all else and believed in the power of love to overcome even the darkest of moments.

In times of grief, it is important to lean on one another, to share stories that make us laugh and cry, and to find comfort in the knowledge that we were blessed to have had [Name] in our lives. Their love will forever be a guiding light, reminding us to cherish each day and to hold our loved ones a little tighter.

6.6.2 Rediscovering Purpose And Embracing Life's Opportunities

In the wake of loss, it can be easy to lose sight of our own purpose and the opportunities that life presents. Yet, as we honor [Name]'s memory, let us also remember their zest for life and their unwavering optimism. They lived each day with a passion that was contagious, and it is now our duty to carry that flame forward.

Let us embrace the challenges that lie ahead, knowing that [Name] would want us to live our lives to the fullest. They would want us to seize every opportunity, to chase our dreams, and to make a difference in the lives of others. In doing so, we keep [Name]'s spirit alive and honor their memory in the most meaningful way.

6.7 Cherishing Memories: Creating A Lasting Legacy

6.7.1 Preserving Memories: Photographs, Videos, And Keepsakes

While [Name] may no longer be physically present with us, their memory lives on in our hearts and minds. One way to cherish and preserve the beautiful moments we shared with [Name] is by gathering photographs, videos, and keepsakes that remind us of their vibrant spirit.

These visual representations of [Name]'s life can serve as a comforting reminder of the joy they brought into the world. As we leaf through photo albums or watch videos of shared experiences, we are transported back to moments filled with laughter, love, and the unmistakable presence of [Name].

6.7.2 Continuing The Vision And Passion

Beyond tangible mementos, an enduring way to honor [Name]'s memory is to continue their vision and passion. Whether it was dedicating time to a cause dear to them, pursuing a dream they held close, or embodying the qualities [Name] exhibited, we can keep their spirit alive through our own actions.

Let us be inspired by the way [Name] lived their life, constantly striving to make a positive impact on the world. By carrying forward their values, we ensure that [Name]'s legacy extends far beyond their time with us, leaving a lasting imprint on future generations.

6.8 Conclusion A: Embracing Life And Remembering [Name]'s Spirit

As we conclude this reflection on [Name]'s life, let us remember that while the sorrow of their absence may be overwhelming, it is important to embrace life with hope and love. [Name] would want us to cherish the time we have, to live fully, and to spread kindness wherever we go.

Let us honor [Name] by supporting one another through the difficult times, by striving to make a difference in the lives of others, and by always keeping their memory alive in our hearts. In doing so, we not only pay tribute to the beautiful soul we lost but also embody the qualities that made [Name] so special. May we find comfort in the memories we shared and may their spirit guide us as we navigate this fragile journey of life.

6.8 Conclusion B: Embracing Life And Remembering [Name]'s Spirit

As we bring our eulogy to a close, we are reminded that while life's fragility may leave us vulnerable to sorrow, it also presents us with the opportunity to cherish each moment we are given. [Name]'s sudden departure serves as a poignant reminder that life is unpredictable and precious. Let us carry forward the memories, the lessons, and the love that [Name] bestowed upon us, and let us embrace life with renewed appreciation, knowing that hope can guide us through the darkest of times. May [Name]'s spirit forever inspire us to live fully, love deeply, and find solace in the beauty that surrounds us.

7. Eulogy 3 - Saying Goodbye To A Beloved Family Member

7.1 Introduction A: Remembering The Life And Legacy

Losing a beloved family member is an immensely difficult experience, as it is a time of deep sorrow and reflection. I am [Your Name], [Name/s]'s [Your relationship to the deceased] and I am honored to speak on behalf of the loved ones gathered. In this heartfelt eulogy, we come together to celebrate the life and honor the lasting impact of [Name]. As we gather here today, we pay tribute to [Name]'s remarkable journey, their profound influence on our lives, and the cherished memories that will forever remain in our hearts. This eulogy serves as a testament to the love, joy, and inspiration [Name] brought into our lives, as well as a reminder to continue their legacy of compassion, strength, and kindness.

7.1.1 Introducing The Purpose Of The Eulogy

Losing a beloved family member is never easy. It's a time when the weight of grief seems unbearable, and our hearts ache with the absence of their presence. But amidst the sorrow, it is important to reflect on the beautiful life they lived and the lasting impact they had on our lives. Today, as we gather here, we come together to honor and eulogize [Name], celebrating the memories, the love, and the legacy they leave behind.

7.2 Early Life And Background: An Insight Into [Name]'s Journey

7.2.1 Family Background And Upbringing: Education And Career Path

Every remarkable life has its beginnings, and [Name]'s journey is no exception. Born into a loving family, they experienced the joys and challenges of growing up, shaping the person we came to know and love. From their early years, surrounded by the love and support of their family, [Name] blossomed into the incredible individual they became.

As they ventured into the world, [Name] sought knowledge and thrived in their educational pursuits. Their thirst for learning led them down a path that would shape their future and the lives they would touch along the way. Through their career, [Name] not only achieved personal success but also made a difference in the lives of others.

7.3 Cherished Memories: Recounting Special Moments

7.3.1 Childhood Memories And Adventures

Among the many treasures [Name] left behind, cherished memories stand out as precious gems. From shared laughter-filled adventures in their childhood to the bonds formed with siblings that stood the test of time, [Name] knew how to create lasting connections and warm our hearts with their presence. Family traditions, deeply rooted in love and togetherness, unfolded year after year, creating a tapestry of memories that will forever be etched in our minds.

7.4 Impact On Family And Loved Ones

7.4.1 A Loving Parent, Spouse, Supportive Friend And Confidant

In the tapestry of our lives, [Name] held a special place. As a parent and spouse, they showered us with love, offering unwavering support and creating a safe haven in which we could always find solace. [He/She] was not just a family member, but also a dear friend and confidant who walked beside us through life's triumphs and trials, offering a listening ear and words of wisdom.

Beyond our immediate circle, [Name] became an inspiration to generations, leaving an indelible mark on those fortunate enough to have crossed paths with [him/her]. Through [his/her] actions, [Name] showed us what it means to live with integrity, kindness, and passion, leaving behind a legacy that will continue to guide and inspire us.

As we say our goodbyes today, let us remember the wonderful life [Name] lived, celebrating the impact [he/she] had on our lives. While the pain of [his/her] absence may linger, the memories and lessons [Name] left us with will forever be our guiding light, reminding us to embrace life fully, love fiercely, and cherish the moments we have together.

[**Prompt:** Adjust this section as necessary to include family, relatives, friends and other close or notable acquaintances.]

7.5 Achievements And Contributions: Honoring Accomplishments

7.5.1 Professional Milestones And Successes

[Name] was not one to settle for mediocrity in their professional life. They approached their career with passion and determination, achieving remarkable milestones along the way. Whether it was climbing the corporate ladder, starting their own successful business, or making significant advancements in their field, [Name] left an indelible mark through their hard work and dedication.

7.5.2 Philanthropic Endeavors And Community Involvement

Beyond their professional achievements, [Name] had a heart brimming with generosity and compassion. They believed in giving back to the community and actively engaged in philanthropic endeavors. Whether it was volunteering at local nonprofits, organizing fundraisers, or actively participating in community projects, [Name] had an unwavering commitment to making the world a better place.

7.5.3 Recognition And Awards Received

[Name]'s exceptional work and contributions did not go unnoticed. Their talent and dedication earned them recognition and numerous accolades throughout their life. From industry awards to community honors, [Name] received well-deserved recognition for their exceptional achievements.

7.6 Lessons Learned: [Name]'s Teachings And Values

7.6.1 Embracing Kindness And Empathy

[Name] understood the profound impact that kindness and empathy can have on others. They always went the extra mile to make people feel seen, heard, and loved. [Name]'s compassionate nature serves as a reminder to us all to practice kindness and empathy in our daily interactions.

7.6.2 The Importance Of Perseverance And Resilience

Life throws curveballs, but [Name] never let obstacles define them. They taught us the importance of perseverance and resilience in the face of adversity. [Name]'s unwavering determination and ability to bounce back from challenges inspires us to never give up and keep pushing forward.

7.6.3 A Sense Of Adventure And Curiosity

[Name] lived life with a contagious spirit of adventure and curiosity. They embraced new experiences, sought knowledge, and encouraged exploration. [Name]'s zest for life reminds us to step outside our comfort zones, embrace the unknown, and live life to the fullest.

7.7 Celebration Of Life: Reflecting On The Joy [Name] Brought

7.7.1 Shared Laughter And Happy Moments

One thing that will forever bring a smile to our faces is the laughter and joy that radiated from [Name]. They had a knack for finding humor in even the most mundane situations and spreading contagious laughter wherever they went. [Name]'s infectious spirit and ability to bring smiles to our faces will always be cherished.

7.7.2 Hobbies And Passions

[Name] had a wide range of hobbies and passions that brought them immense happiness. Whether it was painting, cooking, playing music, or spending time in nature, [Name] found solace and joy in pursuing their interests. We will forever remember [Name]'s enthusiasm and zest for life whenever we engage in these activities.

7.7.3 Impactful Stories And Anecdotes

There is no shortage of memorable stories and anecdotes involving [Name]. From their adventurous travels to their heartwarming acts of kindness, [Name] had a knack for creating lasting memories. These stories will be cherished and shared for generations, ensuring [Name]'s spirit lives on.

7.8 Final Farewell A: Saying Goodbye And Continuing The Legacy

7.8.1 Expressions Of Love And Gratitude

As we bid farewell to [Name], our hearts overflow with love and gratitude for the time we had together. We are thankful for the memories, the lessons, and the impact [Name] had on our lives. Though we mourn their loss, we celebrate the love they shared, and we hold them forever in our hearts.

7.8.2 Commitment To Upholding [Name]'s Values

Though [Name] may no longer be physically with us, their values and teachings will forever guide us. We commit to carrying forward their legacy by embracing kindness, perseverance, and curiosity in our lives. We will honor [Name] by being the best versions of ourselves and making a positive difference in the world, just as they did.

7.8.3 Carrying Forward The Legacy

The best way to honor [Name]'s memory is by living our lives to the fullest, just as they did. We will cherish the moments we shared, draw strength from the lessons they taught us, and carry forward their spirit in everything we do. Though they may not be physically present, [Name] will forever remain a beloved family member, guiding us through life's journey.

7.8 Final Farewell B: Saying Goodbye And Continuing The Legacy

Today, as we say our final goodbyes to [Name], we do so with heavy hearts but also with a renewed sense of purpose. We carry [Name]'s memory within us, embracing the lessons they taught us, and the love they shared with us. Let us strive to live our lives in a way that honors [Name]'s legacy, by spreading kindness, pursuing our dreams with determination, and cherishing the bonds of family and friendship. Though [Name] may no longer be physically with us, their spirit will forever guide and inspire us. As we bid farewell, we find solace in knowing that [Name]'s love will continue to shine brightly through each and every one of us.

Section 3 - After The Funeral

Once the eulogy has been delivered and the funeral has concluded, the journey towards healing and acceptance commences. If you have reached this point, you have already overcome a significant obstacle on the path to healing. You should take pride in your accomplishment. The task you have completed is crucial not only for paying tribute to the deceased but also for aiding in the healing process of those who are grieving, including yourself.

Your healing journey has begun, and there is much to look forward to. Healing from grief is a unique process for each individual. The following chapter explores what you can expect and provides guidance on how to progress in your healing journey following the loss of a loved one.

8. Healing And Moving On

8.1 Beginning The Process Of Healing

The death of a loved one is one of the most challenging experiences that any of us will face in our lifetime. After the eulogy has been read and the funeral is over, the process of healing and moving on begins. This journey towards healing is different for everyone, as grief is a deeply personal and individual experience. However, there are certain common steps and strategies that can help in the process of coming to terms with the loss and finding a way forward.

8.2 Allowing Yourself To Feel

One of the most important aspects of healing after a loss is allowing oneself to feel and express emotions. It is normal to feel a wide range of emotions such as sadness, anger, guilt, and even relief after the death of a loved one. It is important to give yourself permission to experience these feelings fully, rather than trying to suppress them. Talking to friends, family, or a therapist can also help in processing and understanding these emotions.

8.3 Keeping Their Memory Alive

Another important aspect of healing is finding ways to honor and remember the person who has passed away. This can be done through rituals such as visiting the grave, creating a memorial, or participating in activities that the person enjoyed. Keeping their memory alive can help in the healing process and provide comfort during difficult times.

8.4 The Importance Of Self-Care

Self-care is also crucial in the process of healing and moving on after a loss. Taking care of oneself physically, emotionally, and mentally is important in order to cope with the overwhelming grief that accompanies death. This can include eating well, getting enough rest, exercising, and seeking support from loved ones.

8.5 Patience In Grieving

It is also important to give oneself time to grieve and not rush the healing process. Grief is a natural and normal response to loss, and it is a process that cannot be rushed. It is important to be patient with oneself and allow for the ups and downs that come with grief.

8.6 Community And Belonging

Finding a sense of community and belonging can also be helpful in the healing process. This can include joining a support group, participating in community activities, or connecting with others who have experienced similar losses. Having a sense of belonging and support can provide comfort and solace during difficult times.

8.7 New Routines And Meaning

Creating new routines and finding meaning in life after a loss is another important step in the healing process. Setting goals, pursuing hobbies, and finding joy in everyday activities can help in moving forward and finding a sense of purpose after the death of a loved one.

8.8 Seeking Professional Help

Finally, seeking professional help if needed is important in the healing process. Grief can be overwhelming and it is okay to seek help from a therapist or counselor if the feelings of grief become too difficult to manage on one's own. There is no shame in seeking help, and talking to a professional can provide valuable support and guidance in the healing process.

8.9 Conclusion

In conclusion, healing and moving on after the loss of a loved one is a challenging and complex journey. It is important to allow oneself to feel and express emotions, honor and remember the person who has passed away, practice self-care, give oneself time to grieve, find a sense of community and belonging, create new routines, and seek professional help if needed. By taking these steps and strategies, one can navigate the difficult process of grieving and find a way forward towards healing and eventual acceptance.

Frequently Asked Questions

A. Writing The Eulogy

A.1 Can anyone contribute to the eulogy?

Yes, absolutely. The eulogy is an opportunity for friends, family members, and loved ones to share their personal memories and reflections on the deceased's life. If you would like to contribute to the eulogy, reach out to the person organizing the service or the individual designated to speak during the ceremony.

A.2 How long should the eulogy be?

The length of the eulogy can vary depending on the traditions, preferences, and time constraints of the memorial service. Generally, a eulogy is around 5 to 10 minutes long, allowing enough time to capture the essence of the deceased's life and impact. However, it is important to remember that quality matters more than quantity. Focus on sharing meaningful stories and heartfelt messages that truly honor the deceased.

A.3 Can I include humor in the eulogy?

Yes, incorporating lighthearted and humorous anecdotes can be a beautiful way to celebrate the joyful moments and unique personality of the deceased. However, it is essential to strike a balance and be mindful of the overall tone of the service. Ensure that any humor is respectful and appropriate for the occasion, keeping in mind the feelings of the grieving family and attendees.

A.4 Is it necessary to follow a particular structure for the eulogy?

While there is no one-size-fits-all structure for a eulogy, it is helpful to have a loose outline to guide your speech. Consider including sections such as an introduction, sharing personal memories, highlighting achievements and contributions, discussing the impact on family and loved ones, and concluding with a heartfelt farewell. However, feel free to adapt the structure to best reflect the unique life and relationship you shared with the departed.

A.5 Should I include and read the section headings when giving a eulogy?

When giving a eulogy, deciding whether or not to read section headings is important. Reading them can help speakers stay organized and provide structure for listeners, but it may also make the speech seem too scripted or formal, detracting from the authenticity and emotion of the eulogy. The choice should be based on what feels most authentic and meaningful for both the speaker and the audience.

B. Information For Funeral Attendees

B.1 How can I contribute to the departed's memorial fund or charity of choice?

Please refer to the chapter for information on how to make contributions to a memorial fund or the charity that was dear to the departed's heart. It will provide details on how you can donate and ensure that your contribution goes towards honoring the deceased and their legacy.

B.2 Are there any upcoming events or gatherings to honor the life that was lost?

For information on upcoming events or gatherings to honor the deceased's memory, please check the [Resource] for any listed memorial services, commemorations, or events organized by the community or loved ones. It will provide details on dates, times, and locations where you can join others in paying tribute to the departed.

B.3 How can I share my personal story or memory of the deceased for inclusion in the [Resource]?

If you would like to share your personal story or memory of the departed to be considered for inclusion in the [Resource], please reach out to the [resource's author] or the designated contact person mentioned within. They will provide you with instructions on how to contribute your story and ensure that the deceased's impact is properly represented.

B.4 Can I purchase a commemorative item or keepsake in memory of the departed?

For information on commemorative items or keepsakes in memory of the departed, please refer to the [Resource] for any provided details on how to obtain such items. It may include information on official merchandise, memorial plaques, or other tokens that can be purchased to honor the departed and keep their memory alive.

C. The Eulogy And The Healing Process

C.1 Why is delivering a eulogy important in the healing process?

Delivering a eulogy provides an opportunity to express grief, honor the life of the departed, and find solace in shared memories. It allows us to reflect on the impact the person had on our lives and to celebrate their legacy, fostering healing and closure in the grieving process.

C.2 How can I gather memories and stories for a personalized eulogy?

You can gather memories and stories by reaching out to family members, friends, and loved ones who knew the person well. Conduct interviews, ask for personal anecdotes, and encourage others to share their cherished memories. This collaborative approach ensures the eulogy captures the essence of the individual and reflects the collective experiences of those who knew them.

C.3 How do I address the pain and offer comfort in a eulogy?

Addressing the pain and offering comfort in a eulogy can be achieved by acknowledging the difficulties of grief and loss. Share personal reflections on the impact of the sudden illness, express empathy towards others who are mourning, and offer words of comfort, hope, and healing. The eulogy should create a space for collective healing and provide solace to those in attendance.

C.4 What if I find it difficult to write a tribute or express my emotions through words?

Writing a tribute can be challenging, especially when emotions are overwhelming. Take your time and be gentle with yourself. Consider seeking support from others, such as close friends or family members, who can help you brainstorm ideas or even write the tribute together. Alternatively, you can explore other forms of expression like art, music, or creating a visual collage to honor your loved one.

C.5 What role do rituals and symbolism play in a meaningful eulogy?

Rituals and symbolism can add depth and meaning to a eulogy. Consider incorporating rituals, such as lighting candles, sharing symbolic objects, or inviting others to contribute to a memory jar. These gestures can create a sense of sacredness, foster connection, and provide an opportunity for mourners to actively participate in the healing process.

D. Dealing With Memories And Emotions

D.1 How can I cope with the sudden loss of a loved one?

Coping with sudden loss can be an overwhelming and challenging experience. It is important to allow yourself to grieve and feel the full range of emotions. Seek support from friends, family, or a therapist who can provide comfort and guidance during this difficult time. Engaging in self-care activities, such as exercise, journaling, or spending time in nature, can also help in the healing process.

D.2 How can I honor the memory of a loved one who passed away suddenly?

There are various ways to honor the memory of a loved one lost suddenly. You can create a memorial or tribute, such as a photo album, a dedicated webpage, or a charitable foundation in their name. Engaging in activities or causes that were important to your loved one can also serve as a meaningful way to honor their legacy. Additionally, sharing stories and memories with others can help keep their spirit alive.

D.3 Is it normal to feel a mix of emotions, including hope, after experiencing sudden loss?

Absolutely. It is completely normal to experience a wide range of emotions following the sudden loss of a loved one. While grief and sadness may be predominant, it is also possible to feel moments of hope, optimism, and even inspiration. These emotions can stem from the love and connection shared with the departed, as well as from a desire to honor their memory by embracing life and finding meaning in the midst of loss.

D.4 How can sharing memories help in the healing process?

Sharing memories allows us to celebrate the life of our departed loved ones and find comfort in the recollection of cherished moments. It provides an opportunity for reflection, connection, and emotional healing as we share stories, anecdotes, and experiences that keep their memory alive.

D.5 How can I preserve memories in a meaningful way?

Preserving memories can be achieved through various methods. Some common strategies include writing in journals, creating scrapbooks or photo albums, making digital archives, recording videos or audio messages, and even participating in memory-sharing ceremonies or events. Choose a method that resonates with you and allows you to capture and cherish the memories in a way that feels most meaningful.

E. Grieving And Moving On

E.1 How can I find solace and joy amidst the sorrow of losing someone to sudden illness?

Finding solace and joy amidst sorrow is a personal journey, but there are several strategies that may help. Embracing joyful remembrance by focusing on happy memories and cherished moments can bring comfort. Engaging in activities that celebrate their life, such as creating personalized tributes or participating in rituals of remembrance, can also help in finding solace and healing.

E.2 Is it normal to feel a mix of emotions when grieving the loss of someone to sudden illness?

Absolutely. Grief is a complex and individual experience. It is entirely normal to feel a wide range of emotions, including sadness, anger, guilt, or even moments of joy when reminiscing about the person's life. It is important to give yourself permission to feel and process these emotions in your own time and in your own way.

E.3 How can I navigate the grieving process with the support of my community?

Seeking support from your community can be incredibly helpful during the grieving process. Reach out to family, friends, or support groups who can provide a listening ear and understanding. Sharing stories and memories, attending memorial services, or participating in community events can foster a sense of belonging and provide comfort in knowing that you are not alone in your grief.

E.4 How can I keep the memory of my loved one alive while moving forward with my own life?

Keeping the memory of your loved one alive is a personal and ongoing process. Find ways to honor their legacy by engaging in activities or causes that were important to them. Consider creating rituals or traditions that commemorate their life, such as annual memorial gatherings or participating in activities they enjoyed. Additionally, finding ways to incorporate their values and teachings into your life can keep their spirit alive while also allowing you to move forward and find hope.

E.5 How can memories help in the grieving process?

Memories play a crucial role in the grieving process by allowing us to connect with the essence of our loved ones. They serve as a source of comfort, healing, and inspiration. Memories provide a way to honor the lives of those we have lost, keeping their spirit alive in our hearts.

E.6 Is it beneficial to share memories with others who have experienced a similar loss?

Absolutely. Sharing memories with others who have gone through a similar loss can create a supportive community, providing empathy, understanding, and validation. It allows for the exchange of stories, experiences, and emotions, providing comfort and a sense of connection in the midst of grief.

E.7 What can I do to support someone who is grieving?

Offering support to someone who is grieving can make a significant difference in their healing process. Be present, listen without judgment, and provide a safe space for them to express their emotions. Offer practical help, such as assisting with funeral arrangements or everyday tasks. Most importantly, respect their unique grieving process and be patient with their journey.

E.8 Are rituals and ceremonies important in the farewell process?

Yes, rituals and ceremonies hold great significance in the farewell process. They provide structure, meaning, and a sense of closure. Rituals can be personalized to reflect the values and beliefs of the departed, and they offer an opportunity for all involved to come together, pay tribute, and honor their life. These rituals help in finding solace, healing, and embracing the legacy of our dear friends.

E.9 How can I cope with my own grief while supporting others?

Coping with your own grief while supporting others can be challenging. It is essential to establish healthy boundaries, prioritize self-care, and seek support from friends, family, or professionals. Practice active listening and empathy, but also allow yourself the space to grieve. Remember that supporting others does not mean neglecting your own healing process. Seek a balance between comforting others and taking care of yourself.

Other Books/Ebooks In The (Eulogies: From Grieving To Healing Series)

Eulogies When Natural Disaster Takes Our Beloved: Writing Guidelines, Examples And Templates (ISBN-13: 978-1-960176-19-6)

Eulogies When Violent Crime Takes Our Beloved: Writing Guidelines, Examples And Templates (ISBN-13: 978-1-960176-18-9)

Eulogies When Christmas Becomes A Time Of Loss And Grief: Writing Guidelines, Examples And Templates (ISBN-13: 978-1-960176-17-2)

Eulogies When Accidental Death Takes Our Beloved: Writing Guidelines, Examples and Templates (ISBN-13: 978-1-960176-16-5)

Eulogies When Long-Term Illness Takes Our Beloved: Writing Guidelines, Examples and Templates (ISBN-13: 978-1-960176-15-8)

Eulogies For Those We Lost To Sudden Illness: Writing Guidelines, Examples, and Templates (ISBN-13: 978-1-960176-14-1)

.

www.ingramcontent.com/pod-product-compliance
Lightning Source LLC
Chambersburg PA
CBHW030026290326
41934CB00005B/506